Misplaced Vegetables

Poems by

Rich Ives

Copyright© 2021 Rich Ives
ISBN: 978-93-88319-87-4

First Edition: 2021
Rs. 200/-

Cyberwit.net
HIG 45 Kaushambi Kunj, Kalindipuram
Allahabad - 211011 (U.P.) India
http://www.cyberwit.net
Tel: +(91) 9415091004
E-mail: info@cyberwit.net

Printed at Repro India Limited.

Acknowledgements

Burningword Literary Journal: The Secret

The Telegram Got Larger

Drunk Monkeys: Building Materials

Ibis Head Review: What Feeds the Dawn but Darkness?

Indefinite Space: Varieties of Interference

Innisfree: My Neighbor's Car Garden

Poetry Quarterly: Reluctant Weather Report

My Fish Hawk Brings Me Dinner

The Puritan (Canada): A Large Seed from the Old Forest

Ray's Road Review: From the Forest

Sierra Nevada Review: Portions of an Ancient Misunderstanding Rotated on an Immense Carnal Axis

Spillway: Definitions Occurring During Efforts to Determine the Role of the Primary Domicile in Contested Divorce Proceedings

Straight Forward Poetry: A Platter of Meat within a Greater Context of Uncertainty

A Cautious Map of the Garden

Pepper Doesn't Need to Sing

Sweet: Was That Only Yours?

Weirdyear: The Day Before Zero

Contents

Crooked Tree

nobody knows where the mystical trees are
so I can still see them

one path lies upon a thousand
I travel them all with a single pair of feet
and suddenly as I notice a mosquito upon my knee
they are my own

once or twice I was all there was

*   *   *

it's not obvious why the rock doesn't speak
I've never been to the wonderland

so I bought you the mountain
the owner had recently died again
but I forgot to bring it with me

perhaps there's a stone that could tell me
why I'm here and take more time than I have

*   *   *

I live in a crooked tree
someday I'll live in a crooked chair

swallow your goat cheese
the emperor's messenger

wants you to say your nothing
a little louder

what are you doing in your old age but
looking for it

your eyes will be too busy to decide where you're going

*   *   *

fate: I don't want to be reminded
how the old man beat me with my cane

A Walk Before Dawn Gently Sneezes

If daylight's bright cobbler has not killed his wife again,
I'll celebrate my late Thanksgiving. If another fleeting sunset
has not drained away all the reasonably pretentious color,
I'll make of the darkness my gradual celebration.

Everyone kneels and opens the same private door,
so the moon begins pumping its sacred renewable fluids.
They arrive like endless guests with boundary issues. This night
climbs through the opening, letting even greater rivers in.

Another sleeping village knocks on the wet door.
The blossom I put in ordinary water yesterday
is already on its way home, where its siblings shine.
I don't even try to recover the fragile lamp.

Autumn kneels and shivers across the leaf-strewn
dry-brush painting, remembering the same water it drank
last Spring and perspired away into the clouds
during the heated summer. The touch is agonizing,

and the touch cannot get deep enough for this different
desirable kind of affectionate wound. Sometimes my thinking
drifts off into someone else's thinking. Explanations
are one-sided, but implications are often shared.

My shoes' greatest dream is as small as a hazelnut.
There's no one left who can fix it in his dreams, so
I crack it open. I plant it. A fickle litter of hope
arrives with new fevered shoes.

Advancements in Learning Theory

Don't take your superiority to others too
seriously. If you're really smarter, you can see
meaning in their thoughts and actions
that they cannot. Appreciate it.
Not all wisdom is conscious.
Like animals, we all have
instincts and abilities
that let us live well
beyond thought.

I'd prefer talking to three guys with stone tablets in a cave
or three elderly women with poodles at Starbucks.

Quantified Knowledge Acquisition: Theft
isn't the problem unless the discount is guilty.
What kind of an education is shopping?

Now it seems we are leaving evidence all the time.
Too bad the real crime isn't important enough to investigate.

A lie is not a lie when the question is wrong.

Cinderella's Prince

one wart is a temptation
two warts is a gift
three warts is a miracle
if you can't rejoice
admit deception

(the worm knows
which apple tastes the best
why should you settle for less)

put me in the car before you
drive away from yourself
I didn't like you either

maybe we have something in common

The Secret

I was busy criticizing a rock

a gardener with a little slug funk
dripping from his angry shoe

I'm between accomplishments but
the cast-off river has its own explanations

necessary things are not always beautiful

the privileged ocean's temporarily illegible

there is nothing else to say about not saying

pessimism: the body's half empty
optimism: the coffin's half full

at the end of the journey a talking goat
he doesn't have anything to say

I can't sleep some nights it rains all day
a common man doesn't want common things

something will happen of course
but I'm stopping now

only an opening whose words contain
mouths

it makes the first page read right into the last

I can't remember what was said to make me feel this way
but knowing a secret exists makes it less secret

Ode to the Ordinary

The miller kept the fire going
in the stone house of abandon,
ground it down to sparks and ate,

as if his mind were still filled only with
unlikely donkey-house devices of surrender
and entirely intellectual insemination.

Outside fresh millers were hung
bleating from the aging game, the one
the hunt brought back from the wild,

and the wilder taste brought back
wilder ideas and dinner satisfactions,
visitors with too much spare time.

We might assume his house was built to allow
his entrance among ordinary slope songs
and tall walkers of verbal surfaces.

You couldn't describe that man with a pencil
or even the wife playing at playing dress-up,
their performances uncomfortably beyond words.

The state objected to dead girls, but the objects
stated dead girls are no more than us and entirely
lethal if hunting matters anymore. Back then

to the forest for some ordinary suffering,
where meat's perplexed enough to share,
and the miller still keeps the fire going.

Sustainability

In the forest all movement fits a purpose.
If something is only passing through,
it could be dinner, or a disaster. Everything
seems to be in the right place. If it isn't,
I shoot it. Then I'm not in the right
place, but what shoots me?

I have a theory of vegetables in which
I'm on the sidewalk between one empty lot
and another empty lot. I'm moving slowly.
It's the walk we use for gathering, but
I don't know what I'm gathering.

Tragedy always used to end with death.
Now it begins with life. Why does
the hidden part seem closer to the truth?
How deep the roots of the unnecessary tree.
How shall we endure our humanity?

The Mayor's New Policy on the Distribution of Urban Garden Produce

beans are merely color-blind carrots
with a bad sense of direction
and less reason for nudity

carrots are beets with dropsy

beets are round scars made from undiscovered
globes of beaten mud choirs how often
a small mind has nothing to do
but look for itself

clouds and mud
who gets to hold the water

clouds and mud and people
who gets to spill and who gets to squeeze

lettuce is the dream gift of people with wooden teeth
you have to be careful not to let love get too dry
as if the conclusion might curl away like
the damp paper upon which it was written

potato folders cluster beneath main street
appear bone-shocked and cobbled in the light-brown
skull-swaggering distance between one cloth
and another saddled up here we go now

what's aphasia says the aphasiac

pace yourself is not good advice
for a political bullet

Substance

1

the illicit substance begins with separation
gathers differences to share with undesirable possibilities
it fits in a shoe or a toothache an experience of initiation

the illicit substance assembles breakage
as if repair were a capacity of tears
and growth hung on fallen limbs

darkness falls to the apex and toothy
aberrations of symmetry
appear to sharpen the shade

the substance is not quite illegal
but arrests you in your progress towards other
substances

you may borrow from initiation
but you may not pay it back ask for
anything it will give it once then
begin loaning

probability allows the substance
margin of error which is called survival
you must become the margin of error

character allows you
to sink further fortitude
delays inevitability but you

arrive quickly at survival
if all your resources
drained you

2
my chances are the mistakes you make
there is no river of fire only ashes
and more ashes

my people are grasshoppers
my people are snakes who eat the grasshoppers
who are my other people who also feed the hawks
that eat the satisfied snakes

I was speaking pebble after pebble
good solid words with a history of stone
and wisdom came crunching along
quite naturally and everyone listened
as if they were marching to battle

The Motion on the Floor

I wish to speak of the wrist where the wound broadcasts tender-
ness
and escape. Start with a button too big for its hole
and break that, something you wear loosely snaking down.

If you are already playing video games in the bedrooms of the saints,
consider the children digging children out of the hillside.

Reasons for the police to begin crying:

1) one kettle of gizzards one bottle of bile
2) the music starving and moving faster
3) the whisper of prescription armies
4) a toad's measure of aging yogurt

because you could do this a long time without doing anything.

The motion on the floor
was tabled. We called it love,
an angry magician with a sleeve full of tacks.

If the saints are still children, let them suffer as children.
Start with a hole too big for its button.
Start with an ordinary tenderness.

The Telegram Got Larger

every room in the sentence was a new color

I had trained these wolves
and I knew how to defeat a bear
I worshipped indecision

my daughter can pluck out all the eyes in a room

everything is hungry here
the meals are not spaced evenly
and the legs of a table can lead you on

we were some kind of violation so we had to quit ourselves

it's like the door to the middle of a missing universe
it lives in the attic but once it's opened
it cannot close

we were healing but we could have called it sex

she appeared to be one of those gummy
sentimental things fat and unreasonably relieved
encased in a pink snowsuit that made her look like she floated

he kicked the step again and hurt my foot again

learning disabilities
tiny birds between his teeth
something brittle and transferred

I could not partake of the nontransferable emotions

one gooey personal shipwreck
if only I knew what to do with lost ponds
near the dacha on the Red Sea with Petrov

now tell me the color of absence

Thus the Task May Become Limited

bad teachers expect you to memorize deserts good teachers do not
go to conferences in Las Vegas or Wichita or Atlantis

bad students do not know that only ignorance
can contain the good students others pretend to be

a good teacher would adore a bad teacher for
freeing them but there are no good teachers

the children of especially bad teachers sometimes learn from
their parents' mistakes and become better bad teachers

there are no bad teachers where death is the lesson
as in a first fish bowl or a last jar of oysters

alas the bad teacher does not exist for you alone you cannot
give one away or tie one up naked in your glass wagon

the best bad teachers still visit after expiring
and want to know how much they have contributed

there is really only one student appearing everywhere
in disguise this poem is a student and the word "student"

bad teacher etiquette is the same as good teacher etiquette
just remember that growing up is like winning a toad

good teachers are not responsible for their actions
they merely elaborate childhood but the bad teacher learns

bad students know there are no good teachers and good students
know there are no good students either only curious bystanders

go home now if you have learned the way if you can find it
outside the schoolroom and wait for the greater knowledge

when you're the only one missing you can be pretty sure
the bad student will teach you how to use your absence

unless you are the worst student in which case you had
everything the teacher needed before you began to cross the desert

The Journey Tree

The homeless moon wanders the one path.
Fool! You don't have to travel to go farther astray.

You knew how to make a glance precious
and ideas a waste of time.

You were the leader. Love followed,
but how often love leaves you behind.

Now who can claim the fur sheltering the cold heart
is just as warm on the outside?

Only the cloak of ordinary darkness shelters
the abbey from desire. What do I care for words?

The roots are hard and twisted,
but the branches sway crazily in the wind.

When your body moves away from limb to limb,
will the bent ancient donation recognize the gifted?

The Gift of Reason

still considering the wrong distance
I walk among the unknown with my candle
and know that they cannot see me

I've come to the end says the snail
and goes on leaving itself behind

even the barbarians quail at the fouled nest of religion

stick to the trees my shadows
where I am going will eat you

blame as well as praise sleeps restless in youth

the riverhouse stretches to the sea
and all who live there find home a large occurrence

a dispatch chasing the Autumn wind

the forlorn wait tethered
as if their raft had melded to their misfortune
but at least there's still the river

the limpid clock drips patience
the way the cold seeks out the pale scar
I offer you my staff before you need it

wait
the wet slap of washing blocks

pull the cloud cord
a slave to an addiction finds his freedom there
looking elsewhere chains him to progress

I'll share my figs with the ignorant fish

The Cloud Weasel

It seems at once superior and ethereal,
a blue head swaying to the silence of blankets
equipped with insurrection devices and unlimited vertical pastries.

Russet tongues hang like dried leaves from its earth-bound children,
their selection of wallpaper questioned by the contributing trees
as if transparency were more desirable than possible.

So the dogs come running without their brushes,
watery locations of original rescue bestirred
as if talking in your sleep required words.

You can take their little animals along
when you are tiny and your coat fits in your pocket,
which makes the weasel sing, so we never have to ask its name.

The smile, however, is another dimension of poor limb boundaries,
and we seem to go there by ourselves and balance only
the wounded thrill with the chosen adornments.

Such a bold horse might choose to lead a bicycle to water.
No snow has that possible utensil or cocky colored
girls with intelligent feathers to lend.

A whole season of cautionary disturbances still nestles between
going there and arriving at a conclusion as if consequence
were really anything more than the cause of another.

The dream of the overweight badger has been sewn to the risen pillow,
followed by the pillow inhabited by poet A while poet B lives
inside the idea of the cloud badger, which is truly hefty,

followed by the simple hallway of a foreign cave hotel descended
and thereby contained in the shadow of the weasel eating dinner while
the slow badger gets lost in the voluminous curtains of the one
close window,

and then someone's tickets are taken as if presence were not enough
and absence of forethought necessary for true precipitation,
which may contain nothing particularly blue to recommend it.

The Baby's Restless Trousers

his trousers removed from trouserness removed
from inadequate walks to the source of their discomfort
you could say that they were arriving slightly before awareness

some things done professionally don't arrive at their own decorum
all gone says all of the baby without receiving a clear majority
chub sounds still erupted from the baby bundling so lies existed

each cat is named after a bird and an orange
singing in the treetops of impossible sunsets
feathers gallop away with its catless possibilities

baby things were small of course and not done by babies
some of them leaked and voted for change that arrived
for reasons of intense persistent disinterest

if each cat was a bird then each bird was free
to be more than a bird if not less than a cat within
the social skin holding the unintentional religions in

the baby photographs remain birdlike furry babies
couldn't arrive at a sequence of adulthood unsaddled with
responsibilities that behaved like rarified equestrians

blankets with leather escape hatches fell slowly from
invention to occupation and provided minimal resistance
to the directional sleep of the overworked trousers

a rather large pummeled onion conducted us outward
during the snow reversal and toddlers were transferred
to elevated horse chairs until the false crying ceased

it seems brave here to run away from romance quite badly
but if things are really missing they must still be ours
sleep doesn't say anything but we visit with intentions

nearly a dark chalky burden a repentant philosopher's cigar
plump Turkish cigarettes and poultry puffs a mother
could no longer reach for the unlocked door

Unnerved by a Change in the Weather

Each time it rains, fresh clouds discuss
                                    tomorrow
until the surface rises. What reason
can you offer for the drifting

 trees?

Lightning is here in person. Untied by
                                    silence,
I sink into thought. I don't own this anymore,

like always.

Your hand on my shoulder,
my poverty spills out and
                                    travels

alone.

I want to thank you,
but how far is one sky from another.
If you become too
                                    civilized,

you may die.

(Inside that frightened arsonist is a mushroom with flesh melting
into the place where one childhood died. You were only broken,
not empty. (The cold house in the treetops hides its patient story,

folded in upon itself.) Pour the discovered into the discovery, a
lesson tasted by erratic behavior.)

If you could understand yourself,
you'd be more than an occupation,

some grand journal of air traveling with a missing cover.

Small Wagon Full of Apples Pulled by Turkeys

Sleep thought I could hear tomorrow
fussing about in what I was going to say,
but of course tomorrow had gone away.

By the time I had said it, I had to borrow
more today and invent some portion of the future stacked as if time
traveling beneath the simpering woodshed was the more obvious sorrow.

So we stapled the child's vegetables to the child's legs, bare
where there were legs, and its understanding to its
designated head, where there were legs, unlike everywhere.

If you didn't know why you were lost in the mist,
you were more likely to find your way out,
(the way a body still opens and opens, kissed

in its bones and bookmarks, the longer story
slowly reading itself, tasting in earth
something suggestive about resistance)

and the quick-witted ignorance of the confessions
became in that last moment breath-taking,
for the silence required no leaving.

*   *   *

despite arrival at a conclusion
the evening purple with leaving
despite handles desperate latches

despite territories of innocence
borders of luscious guilt
despite compost decay

despite the field
the bicycle swallowing it
despite arrival despite departure

*   *   *

Fundamentally, I'm a pillow without a sleeper,
eleven speed bumps with children playing on their backsides.
Absence invents my suspension, so that I don't seem to be
appreciating my discovery that murder is merely
philosophy with the edges sharpened.

I remain vertical and turn my skin out,
where it accepts me and asks that
I no longer circulate in the same manner.

Because I don't have one, my fresh limp must be yours,
bubbling up to one's head attached, an odorous dance
circulating thoughts to the limbs and trotting happily.

I erupt then something green and reddened.
I sing the hymn for what happened.

Provisions

I'm out of woman now.

The moon's little town ghosts up,
swallows too much night and retires.

I ask because melons contain you, and the cart's overflowing,

and pedaled by the scoop of your back,
the one offering keeps cycling down to
the little loose parts separated
on the sexual waters of one.

It's the kind of innocence no man accepts willingly,

or girl with skin pierced by only one gesture.
She wants the fence to happen down
and a thin prayer of rain to swell
among a recessed child.

We're resting now. We're not the ones
who need to do even this. Deliver us,

for thine is the fiber and the duty
and the insult of never. I can't have you

if the knowing be not of union blessed and taken.
By this we know increase and dream,
by this the seed's pleasant blunder.

Portions of an Ancient Misunderstanding Rotated on an Immense Carnal Axis

Prometheus looked for the five stages of grief and found nine
I went looking for the tenth not with a resistance but a swallow

even the boat was a provisional boat

he placed his immaculate sadness on a pedestal of rice
so honest his transparency erased him

first I freed myself from others because
wind applies itself in layers don't choose
rolling a cigarette of patience that smokes itself

I'm not where the rain is
ill-tempered descendent of steam ferries
crossing skin like an exposé

but I'm still the guardian of diesel fumes and uncelebrated carnage

it's the most you can do it's the least
the nest worn open like a history

you must invent the unknown then discover it

from inside such a flaunting the door looks open
leading to a feverish little café of lice and unreasonable leverage
an interpreted world under siege according to the sea

which is visiting and patient beyond belief
because no other end could begin just here beside Prometheus

Mystical Garden with Chilled Waterglass

which arrogant marathon decides it no longer needs the sun
handsomely pointless with the muscles of a saint
a disciplined lifter without fear of reprisal

in this way we approach the hollows
contained in tennis shoes and bird bones
(but not the skull the skull is too handsome)

if we chickadee the air with winged nerves
we may be able to avoid your sex canoe venturing
(where was that globe of delightful meat-light)

if the moon appears bone-light disappears or do we
expect too much from our delicious judges the entrants
whispering Oh honey you're here and here again

struck with a spoon the chime of the glass ice gun
starts surrounding the abandoned baby
leading the pack in designer nappies his skull

not devoid of attractive features but his skull
keeps hiding (we are two points on a continuum
which do not continue) and father

spills from the snapped towel while
nonmilitary concession charts calculate
how long before wrong's gone

you tried very much being alone
you wrote about it and the sentences
were neither alone nor read

but absent in their own loud way

My Neighbor's Car Garden

I have a neighbor whose flexible pearls of wisdom
dumb me down. The patient mirrors of his seeded dreams

have a reason when I'm listening, but every flower breaks new ground,
and the evening lies down. That's one thing. Another has been
gone since

before I started, the more patient neighbor. A rumor, she was
killed by a wall
that couldn't continue being a wall. It fell with patient deliberate ease,

a predetermined accident. There's something beautiful about it
that strikes me like the repetitively mottled lunatic ecstasy of

lungwort in early spring. Like unseasonal harvests of attractive
hornets.
Like feeding eggshells to the chickens. There are sailors born

on the independent ocean who have never known this land. They seem
to be waiting for someone among us where night is still snow

and falls differently every evening, like gently approaching
shadow-brides.
We keep them in the snow room, call it Dementia and set it apart.

We put such experience in pills and keep the pills close. We do
not take the pills
anywhere because Dementia is angry. Her mother does lots of
bad things

and is buried beside the parking lot. There is no building for the
parking lot,
but you can smell the guilty cabbage, the damp necessary
invitations of rust.

My Fish Hawk Brings Me Dinner

It was my misunderstanding,
but I let a drunkard have it. The penalty
used to be tourists. Now they're the rule.

Sometimes the clouds drink too much,
and it all comes back out clean. What a stomach
those arrogant predators have. There's a party

all night long if you care to go looking. Minnows
swarm the shallows like baby torpedo dumplings.
They scatter and tease when you approach.

Kelp sways like a winded beach umbrella
and collapses to a bulb that opens and closes
according to the petulant weather and sun.

Sea turtles act matronly but squirm inside when
you offer caresses. Their sheltered bodies drag them
back to the sea's extraordinary ordinariness.

Their shell store is wet and salty, pleasantly vagrant.
You have to imagine transport, but the hours and variety
are discreetly generous. The sidewalks thick with breakage

force you to pass slowly. Every day the same losses,
and such implausible quantity. Please, my generous error,
can't we walk a little slower? This darkness. My victim.

Modern Grief

comes from the same suggestion of incompleteness
no longer dries on your shoulders sagging
bathes you every evening before naked chess

there's a way-bad dusting gone corky in it

arranges your automobile purchases
challenges qualified assumptions
babies the baby questions you father

there's a cool tall folder of cylindricals waiting

stimulates the disconnected glands
prepares the finger baths for disposal
occupies the space between episodes

there's effortless us in the you no one invented

generates opportunities for disclosure
considers the accidents of certainty
precludes arrival at the full incompleteness

there's a table with leftovers there's an eater

there's a stimulus there's a doing
there's a hulking over there's an embrace
justice drips closer to the perforations

there's a cool tall cylinder of folded evers

there's a shoreline without a dusty lake to delineate
a tasty ordinary arrives with its zone of allowance
each period of acceptable performance awards itself

there's an ancestor dwelling farther from the conclusion

here take this list to the cleaners
come back with another list
it need not be cleaner

Last Night's Crust of Ice on the Pond

this god isn't a thimbleful
or a warehouse where errant
pleasures get stored

there's no one here already and now
I seem to be part of the reason
reason doesn't work

small repetitive waves
stroking until the surface seems
undisturbed

Building Materials

Each year, a little more of my house
is eaten by grass.

The trees help
but spend more time trying
to get closer to the sun.

You never notice till after
the moment when the food's all gone.

I thought a lot about going
before I went, but after that
I thought about eating.

I understand eating,
I devour eating,

and the grass eats and eats,
and the sun feeds me to what I
have been holding back

because eating is a reservation,
a holding of your place, and

after a while, outside the house,
other houses are forming
from sticks and twigs and hunger.

I don't need the sun to see this,
but my house has been a big dead tree.

Come here, then.
Build me.
Many of us live in dead things.

If I Give You the Last of My Rations

I brought home a sack of bones for animal soup.

I'm my own miscalculation.

If I knew I was wrong, I'd be right,
and so much less than myself.

Even the birds spend too much time
inside their intentions, and I have discovered
that people are birds. They don't understand
their flight is a miracle. They don't understand
they're arriving as often as they're leaving,

but until we have a word for it,
it remains only itself. Being more than
your self is a great responsibility,
but it belongs to the one who has spoken.

If you are more than yourself,
you will have a hard time
living only at home.

Inside the flames I found a church.
Inside the church I found wisdom,
carved in the bones of the mice,
who had been trapped by the fire.

I could not read them until the tiny lives were gone.

Because it's unreliable, I understand it,

and suddenly I'm inside myself,
as if a mirror could fold over and melt
without losing the image of itself it still contains.

Epithalamium

I long to be able to say
the only thing older than me
is what I've become.

If you don't intend to listen,
try sleeping with the book open
in front of you, the way life is.

I didn't know that my thoughts were tied
to the shadowy willow until I flooded.
Something drew me down.

And I didn't know I had failed
to swallow the sun until the sun
failed to swallow the rain.

If either of us had belched success,
we might have noticed how ripe,
how fastidious, our fruit had been.

How old then could desire be,
or the sage that followed it, thinking
the sun was not enough of a problem?

The truth is I rarely slept with the sun
though my desire woke me every day.
Alone on the shore I was burnt by it.

Read now with your eyes closed. Don't stop.
There are too many of us without commitment
or the ability to pass through doors.

Do you think only the handle will move me?
How many doors have you failed to recognize?
Our sun dries them up and enters.

My stick seems a useless weapon but pointing
misdirected many a childhood arrow.
For that I no longer need words.

Soon enough you will lift your head,
and there before you will be what I've said,
an arrow, a stick and a bright yellow bride.

Museum of Emptiness

the front and back door
is the same dark blue and
everyone inside loves me
at the Museum of Emptiness
for bringing them hope

but there's only one door
you're out before you're in
perhaps the museum doesn't exist
or are we just there all the time
the one door is always my door

for a brief moment
I am happy to see myself
I should visit this man more often
his museum will always have
room for my donations

you give your touch freely
but the world that contains it
remains conditional

as if you weren't the one
who invented such happiness

Heart of a Cow

Let's say this time children are not
completely swallowing each other,
and their red cow plundering something

delicate behind the bear grass is not
really moving like he meant to push
himself away from himself. Let's say

it's not going to lead to anything, so we don't
have to think about death. Like this meadow,
I too would have a crow for a heart

if I could plant him there, for a crow
grows as he flies and carries himself
to the others I would know,

and I make myself smaller so I can get into
more trouble, and I say *So death/life,*
*life/deat*h as if they didn't know each other.

The crow is not the messenger
but the message, and he must be received
further and further inside to know him.

We thought the animal was dead
when it climbed down below itself
and slept and learned a lesson,

but the children needed to poke him,
and he made a noise like a lawnmower
trying hard not to start work,

and the children stared at
what they finally understood
could have been empty tomorrow,

this annoyed red complainer buried in beef,
and it was not really that cow
but their innocence that got up farting gas

and roared away without them.

From the Forest

this sky seems small enough
to live in if you could ever get there

but today it does not take over
moderate sky

I'm still the passing cloud
that never stops passing

this might be the torture that kissed you
this air so blue it seems never to have fallen

an illness or a rock it's all the same
not a man but a predicament

like an ant drowning in sugar water
or the wrong hair on a bone-bed

no more than a touch at the horizontal door
felt and not heard and opening out

an act of kindness without the kindness
one thing fell away and then no more

abashed: you don't mean anything disgusting
how can I respect you

this refusal feeding on itself beneath the beautiful leaves
without evil good would be merely ordinary

Down River

a river is strong but has only one direction
it's never far from its bed

it tends to hover there
briefly with its bottom touching

I've asked one to visit my pasture
but this confuses my pasture

water should be vertical and soft
according to my pasture so

a river doesn't belong only a sky
could be allowed such a tentative perch

If I Have One More Thing to Say

The shark-people have pearls in their eyes. I sleep
on a little island they surround, which delights me.
If the moon came down, it would be just as small
and see just as much, but it likes everyone looking.

I too would like everyone looking if I slipped away
as often as the heat of a one-eyed cat. Imagine
what it would be like to close slowly, night by night,
and open quickly with such a singular desire.

The sky's a long walk, but I think about it. One big blue
lantern is not enough. I point to the damage. The clouds
have done this to the way I think about the hereafter
and certain endless notions of endless notions.

The shark-people know the sky as another ocean. Perhaps
I could visit them and make a few suggestions concerning
islands, which may look like droopy eyes from behind that
vast lantern of borrowed blue. I suppose I don't have to

bring up Flowering Almonds or the way they satisfy my
need for outrageous beauty and substance. I'm reminded
how a basket of nuts would not require any reminders. If
I have one more thing to say, I don't know what it is yet.

Blue Plastic Pony with a Long Pink Mane

he tried breathing only twice a day to honor the sea
one last grand footstep before dawn

because sometimes he felt observational
as if he lived in the territory but didn't perform the deeds
as if violence were only thoughts undeferred

all the doors were locked to keep the sky out
but paired doors floated down like cloud feathers
and opened like the wings of a standing bird

the danger was in knowing what you thought because
something larger than itself would not go away

I gathered some vittles I pumped some varmints
no one was at home inside the hallway
which extended a tall full breath seaward

candlelit questions of residence and disengagement created
contradictions gathering him in like pebbles on a beach

if you break it once it gets smaller if
you break it twice it's a principal and gets larger
if you break it three times your imagination is no longer yours

Telegram for a Stranger in Atlanta

I've been living in a message about innocence
doubly removed from unwitting decision

but already you have seen what birds do
and wondered if that could happen

a kind of parenthetical understanding
of irrepressible objects in motion

and something was happening in the message
which could not happen outside the message

creating an atmosphere of plausible unreality
a flight as expectant as Christmas in the south

we didn't trust it because messages were given to us
like favorite flavors they must be better than other messages

but of course they weren't and often revealed
the shallow experience and thought and taste of the sender

but in the message about the message there is no tiny harpsichord
softly imitating the hollow in a bird's bones

and when the innocent message begins dropping words like
breadcrumbs
the unnecessary ones become invisible as if eaten by birds

fly away then wingless innocent there's nothing here
that needs you to pretend more than words

look at them now sitting on thin paper with so little between them
as if a tree melted to white landscape could hold such an
arrangement of

knowing without knowing how to forget and let it happen
as if uncelebrated winter too could fly away with us

Blossoms Opening Slowly in the Falling Evening

1.
The only innocence left
softens in the horn of the bloom's tender.
Shadows blanket the paws of this evening.
Each shovelful of tomorrow fits gently
into the grave of today.

When the night finally arrives with his dark eye,
he removes it and holds it closer to each moment he cannot see.

2.
Whatever a body discards without making a decision,
that's perfume,

the way a color as blatant as a bordello makes you sure it's okay
to take it.

Appreciating yesterday makes you forget today.
Appreciating tomorrow makes you an over-achiever.

Every imagined moment remains thirsty
longer than it remained imagined,

sheet music naked in a French collage
or stuffed in a piano bench where
its purpose remains potential.

3.

The mouth of a creamy flower—
a lily spilling something beyond itself

where a darkening gray fedora is not a hat but an idea
delicious with decadence or

a string of the first wife's pearls
falling across the virgin's collarbone.

4.

I was in a cheap white body.
The suit was linen and barely covered
my cheaper intentions.

I couldn't stop touching them.

An Adoption

We all knew this should happen.
I was thinking about the green dad.
What a budinsky, that insulated wallet-head.

Carlo's shoes behind the drapes are empty,
but everyone thinks he's watching. In town
he's dancing with a tiny whore. She's
rubbing him with palm oil and laughing.

You're limited to fruit now, but once
you were nuts, he says, and, *When no one's
working on nothing, nothing doesn't get done.*

He's an accomplishment, a creature
so important he could drown in a drop of dew.
Carlo says, *Give away your bed if you want to sleep.*

Carlo says, *I crashed my whale into a turtle and broke it,*
the pain nearly tongue-tied and sleeping in its own excess.

Carlo's turtle mother yells at him to come out.
The tiny whore thinks that's pretty funny
even though she could not have heard it.

Carlo dreams up the tiny cubicle of an insect boss,
a pair of typewriters sleeping in a peanut shell,
a stuffed falcon with a needle-thorn beak.
I thought I recognized you.

If there is a name for this, it has time for only
one syllable. Time to have a talk with the spiders.
They aren't going anywhere, caught in their own
intricate traps with too much time on their hands.

A Discovery at the End of an Apple

I found myself one at a time,
and then maybe I was a parade.
That's what I thought, but then,
like a young fire suddenly farting,
or like the beginning of love
when its work is pleasure,
I gave myself away.

Because I was mighty thick, I also wanted to be a tree.

I suppose I should tell you that I thought
you had to subtract infinity to have birth,
and I was not infinity. Had I even been born?

And I wasn't littering. The apple core I threw out the transient
window was organic. I was actually attacking a murderer,
who might be hiding in the ditch and might not even
have accomplished his goal yet and maybe wasn't even

human, which gave me a better chance
to murder him with my apple core,
which wasn't mine anymore, no more
than either death belonged to me.

So now I leave myself behind, and then
I leave what's left behind,
but something is required to do that,
which I can not leave.

By the time a different window appeared,
the door was open, but I couldn't see
why I should leave. So I sat there,

in my vehicle of no more human progress,
driving myself away.

Definitions Occurring During Efforts to Determine the Role of the Primary Domicile in Contested Divorce Proceedings

you're already here now arrive
I've got a plate in my head for you
dinner's late but I'm thinking about
utensils and bargaining with yesterday

before you I could only think about you

three times you did three things and quibbled
up there on top you have a mountain to dig get dripping

transom: the space allowed for thoughts over a doorway

if you weren't already here I'd send for you
you'd be more exciting you'd be potentially misdirected

attic: irregularly shaped storage cubicle from which birds are
separated

three times you performed three actions and fluttered
as if mating were more desirable hovering than submerged

basement: see attic *but with frequent over-boots*
            see leak *as differentiated from sexual behavior*

if I could see you with my fingers
we might enter uncertainty with greater anticipation

eaves: the relation between low-flying clouds and serious elevators
secondarily the operators of such devices

if I could feel you with my eyes
we might live happily upon the two points of a distant mountain

wall: used to link one idea of the experience to another, generally
composed of vertical reasoning and designed to intersect with a
conclusion which sheds rain

something I didn't say must have upset you
will you consume your dinner before departing

door: entry points and access routes to the various parts of the
ordinary vertical thinking used to contain the impression that the
purchaser belongs at any of the various confluence points
created by the desire to leave one part of the thinking and arrive
at another

are you then no longer my reliable husband

The Day Before Zero

1.
The surface of the nervous river rumpled out
as if it had just experienced something illicit,
which it had, although

this time it may have been with
one of its own constituents.

When we arrive at the end, there is nothing,
after which is not nothing but less than nothing
because of what came before,

but is only never having existed truly nothing?

You ran from your mother, who ran from her mother,
who existed for you only as an abstract idea.
Do something.

2.
What were you doing in 1938? seems like a thoughtful question
to me now that I'm old enough to find reason less a reason for
many things I wonder. I've tried often to remember my birth in
1951 because I don't believe anything people tell me. I'm still not
convinced my dead former neighbor isn't historically accurate, dis-
guised as a yellow dog with a festering wound on its nose or a gas
playing with the filament of a light bulb that nervously refuses to go
out.

Right now I'm watching a sock. I filled it with Niger Thistle and hung it in front of the kitchen window, and it's bristling with goldfinch and siskin, but sometimes, I admit, such thoughts have stayed behind and mocked me until I looked off to the side and could see them dancing in the spaces between the ones I hadn't remembered. It's a delicate operation with questionable tools, and not all of my thoughts were so happy doing this, but all of them were doing it.

I'm also listening to the voice of a pebble through the window because of what looks like blood holding on to it before rain washes it, as if I could understand its explanation of the architecture with such attentions. *Blood needs a plan*, I thought.

But I'm not the kind of fool who asks *What is the wind?* and tries to answer without dying. Still, I've noticed I need a little more room to put on my pants now, and I'm wondering what I should offer to recognize the wind's birthday every single day of the year? More obstacles?

3.
Zero is not a number, nor is it an absence.
Once named, it can no longer mean what it is.
It has taken me many years to get to the beginning.
I erase those years. They are nothing. I do not exist.
Now it is possible for you to make me happen.

In the painting, the dead boy is so young and small
that his coffin carriage is pulled by two black-faced lambs
and shaded by a pair of ethereal dove wings, and in
my dream of the painting, which arrives before I sleep,
I remove the glass of water from the dead boy's chest.

We're having a party, and the party is
not having a lot of fun with us, and now
we're celebrating a birthday, but the
day is just getting older and more belligerent.

Memory: If you live long enough you'll want
to do what you used to do without thinking.

You can ask me things for which there are no answers.

Reluctant Weather Report

There's something thrown up that looks like sky
and sticks fallen into piles that deny fire,
but not destruction, and begin again
to feed things that feed things
that rise and look like sky.

There were some bones, and we called them fucking.
There were wings, and we ate them.
The man's lower snout may have been sticking out.

I thought I was a donkey and three kinds of moon.
Floating on the clouds we could not find the shore.
The shadow is a current and ripples over moonstones.

Snow falls trying to get to the other side,
not realizing how the earth clings and transforms it.
Hope evaporates and starts again in the cold,

but sometimes a bird encountering plenty
gets too fat to fly. Up north someone built
a guillotine in the transient woods
and used it to cut off his own arm.

If there was a mule we wouldn't have known
that he wasn't a donkey, but the moon
shone brightly on his absent ears.

Creatures that are not there
can be called residual if they once were.

Their bones may suggest they were eaten,
but fucking falls out like a child.

Up in the sky God's air keeps falling out.
It's very small and numerous,
and it feeds things that feed things.
Sometimes rain participates.
Sometimes sex rumbles and evaporates.

A small stone's hand or breast
will be worn familiar, but our own
stays just a little ahead of us,
which seems more reliable.

A Large Seed from the Old Forest

concerning an epigraph to a poem by Meng Chiao
from Poems of the Late T'ang (A. C. Graham)

Here, eat this, said the wooden boy winning at chess,
and the traveler did, and felt satisfied,
but when he got home, he was a hundred and three.

The windy clack of gossiping bamboo,
their inner chambers crowded with phantoms—
how can you know who has wasted a life?

Look! Your axe handle is rotten, said the other boy,
who was losing, and it was, but it had served him well
and had not failed to split apart the earth from its guests.

By finding yourself right, you gain confidence.
By being confident, you find yourself right.
You might never have to go home.

From out of a mumble rises the right thing to say,
and it is not the thing I wanted to say.
I don't believe I shall say it.

Corn Brides

When is a mime a grave? When is a grave a mime?
Looks to be solid. Looks to be sound. That's the appearance.

Peril in every word. Delight in some. They might be you.
You might be speaking without hunger.

These muscle honey saints stumble bridge to bridge
still employed as a catalyst by Mozart survivalists,

the fetish score of latent furniture
just registered for service.

No kids in the attic. Isn't this breakfast music there yet?

Fine Distinctions

A cat doesn't know where it's going,
but you can see it knows how to get there.

Every stone wants to fly, every bird
to swim, every man to plant his feet
in centuries of stubborn history,

but a man is not made of parts.
A man is one thing that moves with him
and takes too long to discover.

A man is incapable of spilling.
He must place himself outside,
deliberately a part of time.

A dog might appear to spill
wetly, as when hit by a car, but he's
crumbling, and when he's done,
the rug that's left covers his escape.

Out of his eyes come dots of understanding,
out of his backside winds of change.
Imagine him propelled. Imagine him touching.

Just as when a broken man falls apart,
the man does not spill, a woman spills naturally.
A woman can overflow and a new woman
burst those temporary claims—

emperor of cheese then arbiter of cornstalks
arguing late at night in blustery fields of excess,

self-conqueror of maidens without maidenhood,
spider of webs without pretense
marked with body parts and beckoning,

sultan of fierce syrupy intentions
too sweet to be reasonable,

not quite lazy but graceful
in a conservation marshaling motion
gathered unto the profundity of mice
lurking behind mistaken excess.

A cat's friends are lovers and strokers.
They have no aunts, no fathers, no grandmothers,
while a dog's friends are always sibling.

A man transmits the weight of the earth
to his body with each step. A cat
drips into the grass and lifts and
floats along as it follows the thread
that has been set out before it, which
no other one can see or understand.

The fur of that cat cannot be touched.
There is a soft, nearly electric barrier
that satisfies deeply but holds back.
The personal hair sleeps even
as you caress the barrier.

A dog's fur is brash and demands
you try to soften its brittle attentions,
and you imagine you have succeeded
when the dog wags its tail from confusion
as the hairs try to remember what is happening
and make distinctions between them
too fine to fall upon us as difference.

Where the Sergeant Said Mr. and Mrs. Drill Holed Up

The old man's hands were still speaking a silence he had never
given away.

The neighborly wind, pouring birds,
spills out the sky's fluster and flair,
a royalty of mobile apartments.

We must shoot him and order deliriously feathered bird imitations.

Miniature arsonists of the eye, tiny color Nazis—
it's my turn to register dismay, as if
I could be called a poor wedding pattern,
a pair of migratory ideas whistling duck tunes.

Will you imagine a cow grinding its teeth then? Please.

Stunted, the kind ones called me, like a tree worthy
of attention for its difference, or a bicycle you might have traded
for Roberto Clemente's rookie card.

The target, however, is not so easily confused. (This may cast visions
of itself to the side, where the distraction can be used to refocus
the target.)
A direct hit, however, is not a guarantee of excitement, or even a
collusion.

The only comedy here is a broken rib, amusing as ivory.

My fork waited like a girlish soldier—no further legs attached.

A Platter of Meat within a Greater Context of Uncertainty

the birds fly in long flags of sudden intent
they waiver and storm
it cannot end well

there we were visited by the questionable sound
of a boy whistling
the birds alter their course

meat is placed upon the outdoor table
sleep arrives
someone's mountain has appeared through the mist

flies are placed upon the meat
they do not hesitate
a dog arrives sniffing the ground and all available feet

we set aside the photograph in order to see each other better
there might be a match but my pockets are empty

how can you know if what you see is where you are going
someone else's dark glasses soften the approach of the inevitable

the gathering house floats
another innocence
with its feet removed

a gesture that holds itself out

dusty and genuine
as if it belonged to no one

the vast ordinary clothing of daylight falls

A Cautious Map of the Garden

voices wearing leather gloves
direct a leaf to eat and a bird emerges

the weather of eating meat over a campfire has arrived
weather of spiders quivering happily in their beds
with dinner all wrapped and waiting

my words too have eaten other words
and held them captive to deceptive purpose
I have more than toes in my wandering shoes
I have even deceived myself

the pasture of plenty is littered with ripe turds
but it's the combustible dried ones that offer
to keep the fire burning and warm the battered soul

these tears without sorrow belong to Neruda's onions

the ones that need no wings
that can be seen in the dark
that find the missing door
and do not use it

that knock on the vaulted ceiling
of the chambers of the twisted saint
and season our dreams with lunch

the bird that has leapt from the low branch
has the voice of the whole tree

there was a light yellow in the mist
as if it had rubbed against the sun

yes that was a moan you heard
the one stone she reaches for
that looks like all the others
the only word for the stone a map

it must be yours and the dying man's
you don't get one without the other

it's a good thing you're still naked and sweaty

Pepper Doesn't Need to Sing

March: winter's teeth have fallen out
but its jaws work its gums like a trap

pepper doesn't need to sing

sometimes when my big toe thinks
it's a beetle my grasshopper toes get
jealous the little soldiers between
merely impossible wonders

why must the ordinary remain pink
and human while general heal
marches them all forward and lets them
imagine they've been given free will

pepper doesn't need to sing
your tongue does

eventually even a general begins
to consider if the orders are reasonable
if the war is actually fought by soldiers
or by strategists who test their theories

with socks and the periodic removal
of toenails and the excess pride
contained in one road over another
what holds the unit together then

pepper doesn't need to sing your tongue does
good songs are always a little thirsty

but if my big toe were to meet a real beetle
it would most likely have become breakfast
and would in this way march right on out of
the coffin in the belly of its new friend whose

shell bears a surprising similarity to a toenail
with a little more color and a reversible direction
could that beetle be a misplaced thumb or the vehicle
of escape from the general's decaying strategies

pepper's a little dark inside don't be sad about it
good songs are always a little thirsty

private Darkness aim your personal doubts wide
and deep into the flexed rise that holds the flesh arch
stable left to right until forward becomes only the sky
and there's no one but yourself to fight if you get there

April: if you want to fly
learn to make a few mistakes
color them on your eager tongue

Translating Misplaced Vegetables

Carrot is a precipitation funnel for deeper concerns
but rutabaga means my badger is not your badger.

Onion pokes needle bulbs at the leaky meat.
Tender says the nosey air, and arrival is never conditional.

Turnip means I have thought about climbing with my eyes closed,
or the alley is vertical and arrives at your squashed hat.

Squash means indulgence, means relish, means flung to,
ballooned and miscolored, weighing in at let out.

Sweet corn collects its tiny purses full of starch and says,
Stay right where you are and march. I will kiss
each fat little intention and brush you out
to the tip of silk rain yellowing in strands.

Snow peas arrive soup-bonnet green and sweeter than knowing.
Their spiritual cellar arrives celibate, round shaded nuns carefully
listening.

Brussels Sprouts begin limping early, their walking sticks heavy
with intention,
each child clinging to the one vagrant leg vertically aspiring.

A song that repeats itself is a worry, and a worry that repeats is a pea,
for which there is no cause and no excuse and no need.
If you must sleep, choose a small round idea you can't fall off of.

The equivalent is late, and something that light and airy
can crumble from its own weight.

Insects found in the letters between the leaves
punctuate the remarks. Are you still here?
There's no market for the children. Their needs are late
and sing between the lifted stems.

A song that repeats itself is a worry.
If you must sleep, plant a smaller idea.

Troubled and Invitational

The shed's a covered bucket of wasps spilling.

By consequence I mean the endless field stands golden on all sides,
as if deciding to stay had a deathly beauty beyond sky
and brought itself to itself among the insects of thought
that would hurry away with a hunger for difference.

When I claim I know something, I mean if you look without prejudice,
you'll see something that shouldn't have been there, as if one man
had saved our version of the burning library at Alexandria.

But a great hunger for knowledge consumes you
if there is no application to fall upon.

By complication I mean a pouring out of reason and small pinching
that can swell to astonishing proportions and multiply.

By interference I mean if I was a fox I'd answer you.

Standing Next to the Guilty Party, Leaning on Shovels

This last forest is the very place where God lifted me up
and threw me down again
without having done anything else, anything at all.

Some crazy little dark-tempered insects were visiting
and I was further joyfully annoyed
by a couple of substantially ordinary limbs that fell upon me.

Mr. Sticks, Mr. Sticks, what kind of clever test is this
gravitational beating your old leaf boys
have improbably been offering? A single aging tree's

several useless appendages with strength but for
one donation of the father ship have
floated forcefully down upon my own cautionary arm

and suddenly squeezed against bone and colored
my pale and vulnerable surfaces
so that I might look worthy of attention and rest.

I was awarded such affections but once before.
I couldn't use them. Everything
attended without altering appearances and I

was but a detail no relevant one seemed to notice.
The sky is not falling, but I am.
Who can I still ask to place me beneath my sun?

Varieties of Interference

Seasonal lives are not ours. Seasonal lives
are already in ancient progress.

For once tomorrow was not like anything I might write,
which is what the writing had been looking for.

Bring along your temporary haircut, I said, which
tasted like a vision, like a sound at both ends
of a beginning hung on another end
that saved us from ourselves. In another season,

the swaying wheat was sweeping the nervous heated air clean,

as if someone important might walk on it
without knowing the chill of the preparations hadn't ended.

The still winter cold contained nothing
spectacular and immovable, just as
we wished to achieve, just once, and

something you've seen so many times suddenly seems real.

One by One

I thought I was the only one
who thought I was the only one.

There are but two worlds without me,
and neither of you insists. One way
to say this is two ways to deny it.

The containers were here first,
with nothing in them. How did we know
they were containers? We must have
needed to contain something.

I do this right now, with impatience,
thirty years ago.

I'm not saying that's the way it should be.

Ordinary is the way we say
not this day.

You have to listen to understand
what hasn't been said.

A More Useful Approach to the Answer

Let's invite the missing pieces to the empty indulgence.
In this version I may arrive at a happier audit. No taxable profit.

I'm going to be retarding my constitution of coherent plans
that I might accommodate a place of greater removal, yet the
truth I offer

may not be the truth I know. I signed up for Advanced Living
and found myself at a distance, forgetting the nature of nature.

Too soon the unplanned flowerings begin testing us, love
deliveries engineering future flavors on visitors' tongues. Truth

is not a conclusion but what you do with its constituents. The answer
lies off to the side, watching the question struggle. It doesn't know

how to apply itself. It doesn't know it arrives only after. You too
are an answer, off to the side. Go further away now.

A Couple of Things I Can't Explain

The leaves clattering in the wind
is a reminder of all that remains unfinished,
on its way to a new form before it has
finished with the old one. The strain
is colorful and evokes romanticism
in the same way things that bravely die
seem to be starting over before they're dead.
Don't we all long for that experience
that allows no room for tomorrow?

The animal in the man who has been
remembering absences wants to run.
He doesn't know and he doesn't care
when running is after and when it's from.
Running is its own place, and he wants
to get there. The man doesn't understand.
He thinks there is an answer for every
possible choice. He can't just rest inside
the provocative question to understand it first.

From outside the animal, the dilemma seen as
melodrama grows comic despite the death in it.
Inside, there is a muscular need for obstacles,
a restless leaping over things that are missing.
Haven't you ever seen a man react illogically
to something that isn't there? Didn't you know
without even asking the question that he needed
to exert that something leaping inside to get out,
to prove he could overcome emptiness?

Now the leaves are gathering where they will sleep
between small conversations and blustery boasts.
They're not afraid of the rain, but they should be.
It's the obvious weight of everyday weather that
finally drags you down and breaks your stem,
which can feel like freedom in the cold future.
Death too is a freedom, rehearsing every day,
joyous in its pieces and always on the way to
something greater that disappears inside its name.

Was That Only Yours?

Stars speak and the cold January wind
gathers their falling words
and whitens them.

They never say the same thing twice.

Are those your habits
crossing the street against the traffic?
No wonder you say wonderful things I don't believe.

Impulsiveness gets the attention
while wisdom watches
with his clever dog that doesn't bark.

One thought later
there's paradise.

Don't put your foot through the sky.

In everything, I navigate with what humans have done.
Another life signed its mysterious name,
but don't ask me. It's big, too big
to read more than once.

Debt: Throw something away, and it's yours.
Love: Give something away, and it might be yours.
Religion: Follow something away, and it's you.
Childhood: Forget where you're going.

Wisdom: Don't forget where you haven't been.
Happiness: Forget where you wanted to go.

Success: a burning twig
Failure: two burning twigs
Life: three burning twigs

Do you still think the ashes might speak?

What Feeds the Dawn but Darkness?

I made the rain. I designed the fatter drops to flop more gently
and spread like a circus warming up. I'd play by the rules
if I knew what they were. Love's not something to sip at.

He pauses on the path and twirls his cane till it sings.
She slides each hand up the other sleeve. Death is waiting
like cold fresh well water ladled from her bucket.

All water means mischief. It moves beyond its boundaries,
and when stopped, it stagnates and breeds and vibrates between
odors and tiny wings hovering. Ravaged then this territory of sleep.

I know that before I was not empty because now I have spilled
from my creamy cathedral of butter and sin. *I must open you to
my exquisite sadness. You're too happy to believe*, said the lover.

The lake is a polished table adorned with carvings. Two loons and
a scuttle of ducks and suddenly dinner is served. Don't you want
to climb in the boat and row back and forth between courses?

The heart is not the enigma but everything that comes to it.
I'm speaking now to only you, and it's a scattered voice like yours
before I was only thinking of Russian stars on the Neva.

I hadn't known the pleasures of being tired. The weather soaks up
songs, so that repeating them clears the air. How wet is the sunlight.
I know only one poem, and I feed it relentlessly, its fog a dirty blonde.

I made the wind. I can see its road now only as far as the gate, closed as if it had never opened. Light approaches straight from so many rebounds it's crooked and soft, in captivity.

Don't worry. Life is easy. You don't even have to do what makes you happy. The ridiculous thing you said found a place for itself. The brilliant one remains lonely.